AN INVITATION
TO FORGIVE

A Study of the Book of Philemon

MARGARET ARMANIOUS

An Invitation to Forgive

Copyright © 2013 by Margaret Armanious

All rights reserved. No part of this book may be reproduced or transmitted in any form or by any means without written permission of the author.

Unless otherwise noted, Scripture is taken from the Holy Bible, New King James Version®. Copyright © 1982 by Thomas Nelson, Inc. Used by permission. All rights reserved.

Scripture quotations marked "KJV" are taken from the Holy Bible, King James Version, Cambridge, 1769.

Scripture quotations marked NASB are taken from the Holy Bible, New American Standard Bible. Copyright © The Lockman Foundation 1960, 1962, 1963, 1968, 1971, 1972, 1973, 1975 1977, 1995, used by permission.

Scripture quotations marked NIV are taken from the Holy Bible, New International Version. Copyright © 1973, 1978, 1984, 2011 by Biblica, Inc.™ Used by permission from Zondervan. All rights reserved worldwide. www.zondervan.com.

Scripture quotations marked NLT are taken from the Holy Bible, New Living Translation. Copyright © 1996, 2004, 2007 by Tyndale House Foundation. Used by permission of Tyndale House Publishers, Inc., Carol Stream, Illinois 60188. All rights reserved.

Cover image copyright by istock/shaiith

ISBN-13: 978-1494384036
ISBN-10: 1494384035

Dedication

Dedicated to Baba (my wonderful father), for once teaching this great epistle so well that it has inspired my own study.

With Love,

Margaret

Acknowledgments

Special thanks to my editor, Paul Conant, of PWC EDITING for editing the contents of this, my first published Bible Study. You have been a big part of seeing this project come to fruition.

Contents

Introduction 1

1 Encouragement and Accountability 5
2 The Character of One who Forgives 13
3 For Love's Sake 19
4 The Transformation of The One Forgiven 27
5 The Dynamics of Forgiveness 35
6 The Purposes of God 43
7 The Motives of One Who Forgives 53
8 As Examples 63

Discussion Questions—Character Studies 71

Introduction

Can true forgiveness ever be commanded? Can loyalty and harmony come by compulsion? What is the character of someone who forgives, and on what basis do we forgive someone who has offended us? In the book of Philemon, we discover not only the answers to these questions but also the rich Biblical principles on which they are based.

Read the Book of Philemon

Philemon is a very short book of the Bible, just a page or two, found right after Titus and just before Hebrews in the New Testament.

Paul writes this Epistle from a Roman prison (appr. 60–62 AD), the same place he wrote Philippians, Colossians, and Ephesians. It is addressed to Philemon, a wealthy and prominent member of the church at Colosse who became a believer under Paul's ministry several years earlier, probably while Paul was in Ephesus on his third missionary journey. It is apparent that the church at Colosse met at Philemon's home, so he was well known among them (Philemon 1:2).

Philemon happened to own a slave by the name of Onesimus, who stole money from him and then ran away. Because he knew that Philemon had the legal right to kill him, Onesimus escaped to Rome where he met the Apostle Paul and was converted by Paul as well. As one who led Onesimus to Christ, Paul grew to love the runaway slave and took it upon himself to deal with Onesimus's crime. He sought to restore him to his master.

The letter is written urging Philemon to forgive Onesimus and to take him back not only as a slave but now as a brother in Christ. So, with faith that Philemon would do the right thing, Paul sent Onesimus back

Introduction

to Colosse with this letter. Paul also sent his messenger, Tychicus, with Onesimus to protect him from slave-catchers along the way. He also used this opportunity to have Tychicus deliver another letter, which we know today as the Epistle to the Colossians.

By far, the prevailing theme of this little book is the lesson it teaches about the character and motives of one who forgives. We will look at the attributes of one who forgives as we observe Philemon through Paul's eyes. On another level, we will also see the most brilliant and insightful manner by which Paul appeals to Philemon on Onesimus's behalf. Paul exhibits a firm and rational yet loving appeal for their reconciliation.

Besides the theme of forgiveness, some suggest that the book of Philemon is a statement concerning the institution of slavery. You see, at the time of Christ, slavery was a typical part of society. Some estimates figure that slaves accounted for about one-third of the Roman population. Although their masters were known to have unlimited and often severe power over their slaves, by the time of the New Testament, the attitude towards them was beginning to change. There had been some laws passed, and in many cases slaves were treated very well. Realizing that contented slaves were more productive, masters began to be more easy-going with slaves. Many learned their master's trade and were granted the right to such things as owning property, leaving estates to children, and marrying if they wished. Yet slaves were still considered a master's property, and depending on the master, a slave could be subject to severe punishment and even death if he committed a crime against his master. So, while there were abuses, there was hope for abolishing slavery. With the changing mood towards slavery already taking place in Rome, we see that Christianity's approach to the topic of slavery is not a focus on social agenda, but rather a pursuit to change the hearts of those involved. The perspective is that where godliness is seen, be it in a godly husband, wife, superior, or worker, there is an influence on the whole. Thus, what is in the heart changes a nation. This is Paul's pursuit as he made the statement that Philemon's slave was now his brother in Christ.

The Apostle chose wisely to focus on the gospel in his letter, and in so doing, he reminds us all that the morals and order of an upright society begin in the heart. In application, I believe it is always important to do our part to speak up for Christian values in our society through actions such as voting and active civic participation whenever possible. In fact, as Christians, we must do so. However, such activities cannot change someone from the inside out. I believe that had the focus been on social reform, it would have only distracted from the gospel.

What is amazing about the book of Philemon is that such a short letter is so saturated with practical wisdom. Within its paragraphs we see the shining example of godly character, godly bases of persuasion, and insight into human nature. We begin to understand the heart of true motivation and victory over resentment and barriers that separate us. In less than a page of writing, the Holy Spirit uses a simple letter to resonate the principle of grace freely given and freely received.

As you read through the questions in this study, you'll notice some begin with this symbol (♥). These questions focus on life application.

1
Encouragement and Accountability

"Paul, a prisoner of Christ Jesus, and Timothy our brother, to Philemon, our beloved friend and fellow laborer, 2) to the beloved Apphia, Archippus our fellow soldier, and to the church in your house: 3) Grace to you and peace from God our Father and the Lord Jesus Christ."

Paul addresses himself as a prisoner of Christ Jesus. It is interesting that he chooses to identify himself as a prisoner, rather than an Apostle of Jesus Christ, as he does with most of his other Epistles. Why is that so? Many commentaries point out that Paul is not writing from a standpoint of authority here. He identifies himself as a prisoner, as one who is making a huge sacrifice in his life for the sake of Christ. He doesn't state that he is a prisoner of the Roman government, he is a prisoner of Christ. It was Christ's will that put him there, not Rome. He is put in prison for a specific purpose—to evangelize, to write the Epistles mentioned, to suffer for the sake of Christ, and as we shall see—to bring the gospel to a runaway slave. I believe the Holy Spirit divinely inspired Paul to choose each word even from the beginning, already setting the tone of the letter. As John MacArthur puts it, "He is not laying some authoritative message on the church; he is speaking tenderly, personally, warmly, compassionately to a friend. And it is an appeal to his heart, an appeal to his compassion, to his love, so there's no need to refer to his apostolic office or calling or authority" (John MacArthur, *A Living Lesson on Forgiveness*, Transcript of Tape GC 57-1 [1997], p. 5).

Encouragement and Accountability

How do you think Philemon must have felt as he read that Paul was a prisoner of Christ?

_____

_____

_____

Paul was the beloved brother that led Philemon to Christ. Paul brought the light of Christ to Philemon's heart and brought him the message of Christ that changed his life. It may have been a while since Philemon had heard from Paul, and to hear from the great Apostle must have stirred much emotion in Philemon. No sooner than Philemon's eyes moved past the name, he reads "a prisoner of Christ Jesus." Do you think his heart sank at the words? Can you imagine the heartbreak it must have been to hear that someone so dear to him was in prison? Here he was, living in a big house, enjoying his God-given wealth, and the great Apostle, his dear friend, lost his freedom and was living under house arrest. What's more, Paul calls Philemon "beloved friend and fellow laborer." What? Now the great Apostle was calling him beloved friend and fellow laborer? How humbling it must have been to be put as an associate of someone so renowned! As John MacArthur comments, "...what he (Paul) is really saying sort of subtly to Philemon is, 'Look, Philemon, if I can do this for Christ, can't you do this relatively small favor I am about to ask? If I can bear the harder task of being in this prison, can you do the easier task that I'm going to ask you to do, and that is to forgive?'" (*A Living Lesson on Forgiveness*, Transcript of Tape GC 57-1, 1997, p. 5).

An Invitation to Forgive

How do you think this must have affected Philemon's willingness to do what Paul has asked?

_____
_____
_____

♥ Has anyone ever commended you publicly? What was your relationship to this person? How did it make you feel? Did the public compliment affect your behavior?

_____
_____
_____
_____
_____
_____
_____

Briefly mentioned in the greeting is Timothy, not as a co-author, but as Paul's present companion and also an acquaintance of Philemon. Timothy was with Paul in Colosse, and it is he whom Paul often calls his "spiritual son" (1 Tim. 1:2, 2 Tim. 1:2). He was singled out as the one who would take on the role of spiritual leader after him. Others addressed in the opening are Apphia, who was Philemon's wife, and Archippus, who most likely was Philemon's son. We see that he is *"a fellow soldier"* in Christ, so he was not idle in the ministry. Next, we read *"and to the church at your house."* So, it is obvious that

Encouragement and Accountability

this family is active, striving, and influential in the body of Christ at Colosse. They were not complacent, "blend-in with the others" type of Christians. They were in the forefront, active in the body of Christ. And yet, Paul is about to reveal a problem in their household. He wants it known that Timothy is aware of the contents of the letter, and that the letter was to be read to the church.

Why do you suppose Paul indicated that the letter was to be read publicly to the church? (See 1 Timothy 5:20 for some insight.)

_____

_____

_____

First Timothy 5:20 indicates that those who are leaders in the church are to be held accountable to the church. Although we don't know if Philemon was an elder, there is reason to believe that he was prominent in the church. Because he was so well known, Paul wanted his concern for him to be known to his church, so that they may be there to hold Philemon accountable and also be mindful of their own conduct. We all like to go to church to visit and fellowship, as long as people don't start "getting into our business," don't we? We all may tend to keep our "Sunday morning self" separate from our "weekday self," but is that the way it ought to be? Even though it is unpleasant, wouldn't we want to be a part of a church body that cares enough to speak the truth in love, or would we rather be left alone by a church that is unconcerned with our well-being? Paul was lovingly acting in the role he was called to as an Apostle of Christ when he made this issue known. He genuinely cared for Philemon and was doing so *"with joy and not grief"* (Heb. 13:17). I believe Paul strove for accountability for Philemon.

An Invitation to Forgive

So here we already see a brilliant combination of commendation and accountability. It is as if Paul is saying, "Philemon, I recognize and encourage your work. You are a credit to the body of Christ. I want everyone to know that. Oh, and by the way, I want them to also know that to whom much is given much is required (Luke 12:48), and I honor your position enough to call your attention to this issue."

♥ Wow! What if our churches today would more consistently practice such a pattern of accountability? Write your thoughts on this.

_____

_____

_____

> *"...Grace to you and peace from God our Father and the Lord Jesus Christ." (v. 3)*

Paul often inserted these words as a standard greeting in his letters, yet they hold a great impact in application and truth.

What do these words tell us about God?

_____

_____

What do they tell us about Jesus Christ?

_____

_____

Encouragement and Accountability

Grace is the unmerited favor of God. With these words, the recipients of Paul's Epistles were reminded of the grace of God through Christ's death on the cross. What's more, God our Father and the Lord Jesus Christ are the source of grace and peace toward our fellow man. It certainly doesn't come naturally, for what Paul is about to ask of Philemon, he is going to need a lot of grace to take back a stealing, runaway slave.

What else does God our Father and the Lord Jesus Christ provide for us? Peace. Philemon no doubt had some anger towards Onesimus. Slaves cost money to replace, and the money Onesimus stole was a loss and a disloyal slap in his face. Philemon must have struggled with forgiving him, and it certainly would have been more comfortable to be vindictive and angry...or would it? As a Christian, Philemon had the baptism of the Holy Spirit within him (Luke 3:5, Acts 1:38). That means that he had all the workings of the Holy Spirit, including the conviction of the Holy Spirit about sin (John 16:8–11). He had a new nature (2 Cor. 5:17), which surely was at odds with the old nature before his conversion. One thing we can also know is that the Holy Spirit always does His job (Phil. 1:6), and in this case, He was surely prodding Philemon to do the right thing. We can only imagine the spiritual battle within him—and if we are true believers, we can relate to how unsettling it is to remain in disobedience. According to the Word of God, what is the only way to restore peace? It is to be reconciled to God through a change in our own thoughts, agenda, and will (Isaiah 26:3).

On his end, Onesimus had no idea what he faced if he should return to Philemon. Out of fear and perhaps pride, he could have chosen to disobey and run away from Paul as well. Yet, as a new believer, he also had the Holy Spirit within him. Before meeting Paul and coming to conversion, Onesimus must have had a strong carnal determination to betray Philemon, otherwise why would he have left a benevolent

An Invitation to Forgive

and good master? Now he saw his crime for what it was—disobedience to God. He needed the peace of reconciliation between himself and Philemon and to God Himself.

And the Holy Spirit still works in the same way with all his children.

As with Philemon and Onesimus, the Holy Spirit will continue to convict and prod us towards a restoration of fellowship with Himself and with each other (Eph. 4:1–3, 1 John 4:12). Thankfully, with that conviction, we are also given the supernatural ability to do the right thing. We can choose righteousness and have the peace that only God our Father and the Lord Jesus Christ can provide.

How can Colossians 3:15 be applied to Philemon and Onesimus's lives? Do you see how the Holy Spirit would do a similar work in both of them as they are "in one body" (that is, the body of Christ in the church)?

_____

_____

_____

2
The Character of One who Forgives

"I thank my God, making mention of you always in my prayers, 5) hearing of your love and faith which you have toward the Lord Jesus and toward all the saints, 6) that the sharing of your faith may become effective by the acknowledgment of every good thing which is in you in Christ Jesus."

These verses tell us a lot about Philemon. First of all, they tell us that Paul thinks highly of him. There is nothing in Paul's letter to Philemon that is negative about his friend, nothing that Paul sees in error about his character. In fact, Paul is saying that every time Philemon crosses his mind in prayer, he thanks God. It sets a spiritual example to us that we ought to thank God when He accomplishes great things in the lives of others, doesn't it (2 Thess. 1:3, Col. 1:3–7)? It is a compliment to Philemon and also an acknowledgment that God is the source of anything good in him. So, Philemon stands out as a noble and godly man. His character stood out even more than his involvement in the church. Paul tells him he has heard good things about him (v. 5). In the Greek, the phrase **"hearing of your…"** is set in the present active participle, which expresses continuous or repeated action (*The Complete Word Study New Testament Dictionary*, edited by Spiros Zodhiates [Chattanooga: AMG Publishers, 1993], p. 716). Paul is saying, "I have heard and I continue to hear these good things about you." Philemon is consistent and has proven himself genuine, continuing to display these godly attributes.

What are the consistent character traits Philemon displays?

The first is a love and faith toward the Lord Jesus Christ—he is a true believer in the Lord Jesus Christ. He has the indwelling Holy Spirit in him,

The Character of One who Forgives

so therefore he has the ability to forgive. He is one who has the conviction of the Holy Spirit and one who knows what it means to be forgiven.

This is essential. The only way to forgive offenses that the world would say we are crazy to forgive is to have a love and faith in the Lord Jesus Christ. We are all looking to defend ourselves in the flesh, aren't we? It would have been understandable for Philemon to punish Onesimus. The law was on his side. Onesimus was a criminal. But Philemon had a concern and love for Christ, and as a Christian, he was prepared to forgive.

The second characteristic that Philemon displays is a love toward all the saints—Philemon had a love for his fellow believers. The Greek word used in this phrase is "agape" love. According to *Vine's Expository Dictionary of New Testament Words* ([Oliphants Ltd., 1952] p. 20), "This is a love that is proven and shown through action and not just merely words." As described, it "is not an impulse from the feelings, it does not run with the natural inclinations, nor does it spend itself only upon those for whom some affinity is discovered. Love seeks the welfare of all, and works no ill to any. It seeks the opportunity to do good to all men, and especially toward the household of the faith." In other words, it is a consistent and demonstrative love.

Read 1 John 4:7. What is evident in someone who is born of God and knows God?

_____

_____

_____

_____

_____

This Scripture in 1 John uses the same word for love as our study text—*Agape*. This further emphasizes that those who love the brethren love God. Philemon genuinely loved the brethren, and he genuinely loved God. It was not a superficial love. It was a deep and abiding love that was ready to sacrifice for others. It was an unselfish, action-oriented and deliberate love.

> *6) "... that the sharing of your faith may become effective by the acknowledgment of every good thing which is in you in Christ Jesus."*

This is a wonderful passage of encouragement from Paul to Philemon. It displays a third characteristic of someone who forgives: An effectual living out of one's faith. The word "effectual" denotes "active, powerful in action" (Vines, p. 19). The *NIV* (1973, 1978, 1984, 2011) reads, ***"I pray that you may be active in sharing your faith, so that you will have a full understanding of every good thing we have in Christ."*** Paul is saying, "Philemon, I want your faith to continue to be powerful." How is this done? "Through the acknowledgment of every good thing which is in Christ Jesus." The word for "acknowledgment" (or in the NIV "understanding") is the word "epignosis," which is "akin to full, or thorough knowledge, discernment, recognition" (Vines, p. 27). In contrast to the word "gnosis," "epignosis" is more intense, because it expresses a more thorough participation in the acquiring of knowledge on the part of the learner. In the New Testament, it often refers to knowledge which very powerfully influences the form of religious life, a knowledge laying claim to personal involvement (*The Complete*

Word Study New Testament Dictionary, edited by Spiros Zodhiates [Chattanooga: AMG Publishers, 1993], p. 624).

We as Christians know that we are equipped with every spiritual blessing which is in Christ (Eph. 1:3). We know that we are given the fruit of the Spirit (Gal. 5:22–23), and everything we need for life and godliness (2 Pet. 1:3). Yet, to say that we know spiritual blessing by reading God's Word is not the same as knowing the joy of yielding to the Spirit enough to live it out. That would be like saying we know how to play tennis by watching someone play tennis or sitting in on an instructional video. Until we put the racket in our hands, we cannot fully know what it is like to play tennis. Only then can we gain a true understanding of the sport. This is what Paul meant by his statement. Paul is saying, "I want you, Philemon, to continue to be powerful in the sharing of your faith. I want you to know of the good things within you as you live them out. I want you to be aware that they are there as you stir them up."

If we give of ourselves, we experience the joy of giving. If we are peacemakers, we experience the result of peace. If someone tries our patience, we experience the strength of perseverance. If our faith is tested, we find that God is trustworthy. I could name countless spiritual blessings of which this principle can be applied; these are just a few.

❤ Can you relate to the "acknowledgment of every good thing which is in you in Christ Jesus?" Have you experienced any circumstance that prompted you to act upon the knowledge of Christ's spiritual blessing and equipping within you? How would you have assurance had you not obeyed? Please describe.

_____

_____

An Invitation to Forgive

❤ Can you name any more?

_____

_____

❤ What are some spiritual blessings that you "know" (gnosis) you have, but you do not "know" (epignosis) you have?

_____

_____

❤ Like Paul, take a moment to write a prayer about being effective in the next opportunity to share and live your faith.

_____

_____

3
For Love's Sake

"For we have great joy and consolation in your love, because the hearts of the saints have been refreshed by you, brother. 8) Therefore, though I might be very bold in Christ to command you what is fitting, 9) yet for love's sake I rather appeal to you—being such a one as Paul, the aged, and now also a prisoner of Jesus Christ. 10) I appeal to you for my son Onesimus, whom I have begotten while in chains."

Paul points out to Philemon that there is evidence of his love for the brethren. Not only has he heard of it, but he has benefited from it himself. Philemon's love brought Paul great joy. Philemon was the type of person who was an encouragement and not a burden. He was a breath of fresh air to others He was a blessing. He was concerned with other people's well being.

❤ Do you know someone like this?_____. How has this person refreshed you in the Spirit? Can you recall a time their encouragement made a difference in your life?

_____

_____

That's the kind of person Philemon was. He was an encouragement to others, and this passage implies that someone who is concerned about others is one who is more likely to forgive. Paul is reminding Philemon of who he is in Christ *("...which is in you in Christ Jesus")*. Now, I know that there may be some suspicious folks who may be reading Paul's words and wonder if he is being manipulative, "buttering him up," because he wants something from him. I was wondering the same thing, but I have concluded that could not be possible, for the fact that Paul was writing under the inspiration of the Holy Spirit is reason enough to determine that his motives were pure; notwithstanding Paul's general reputation and constant defense of his integrity throughout his Epistles. He was always careful to conduct himself in such a manner as to be above reproach. He withstood criticism, envy, accusations, and opposition from false teachers and kept himself blameless from them. Besides, why would he manipulate Philemon when he could have commanded him (v. 8) to take Onesimus back? He is simply showing his confidence in Philemon's character based on the evidence of this faith. Do you see the gentle way that Paul deals with Philemon? He shows no ulterior motive and makes no demands. He simply tells him what he genuinely loves about him. This leads us up to the next and (what I believe is) an incredible verse:

> *8) "Therefore, though I might be very bold in Christ to command you what is fitting...."*

Paul could have demanded that Philemon take Onesimus back. It was the right thing to do. In fact, Christ Himself was clear in His command about forgiveness, saying *"...if you do not forgive others their sins, your Father will not forgive your sins"* (Matthew 6:15 NIV). Notice that this is a straightforward statement. It is a clear expectation, whether we feel like forgiving or not. I think this brings up a very interesting question:

❤ If we forgive because we are commanded to forgive, how can we be sincere about it?

_____

_____

_____

∞ An Invitation to Forgive

After all, if we are not acting in love, we are nothing (1 Cor. 13:1–3). I believe the key is that as Christians, we have the Holy Spirit within us. He gives us the capacity to forgive (Romans 8:5–6). He is the one that energizes and empowers us to have His mind and heart on any matter, and forgiveness is not an exception. We initially obey, and in obeying, we not only comply with God's command, but we also agree to have our hearts changed in the process.

Turn to Romans 8:5–6 and fill in the blanks:

For those who live according to the _____ set their minds on the things of the _____, but those who live according to the _____ set their minds on the things of the _____. For to set the mind on the _____ is _____, but to set the mind on the _____ is _____ and _____.

As the Scripture above states, I don't believe any act of sincere obedience to God goes without being given the blessing of peace as a result.

> *9) Yet for love's sake I rather appeal to you—being such a one as Paul, the aged, and now also a prisoner of Jesus Christ.*

Paul knew that he could have been more forceful with Philemon, but he also knew that he could motivate Philemon to forgive from the heart by gently prodding him to act in love.

❤ What do we already know about Philemon that would cause us to believe he would respond to what Paul would ask of him?

_____

_____

If Philemon had not shown any signs of righteousness, Paul may have approached it differently. John Calvin describes it well, "…since those who are ready and willing to do their duty listen more willingly to a calm explanation of what is required than to an exercise of authority, Paul has good reason to entreat when he is dealing with an obedient man" (*Calvin's Commentaries: The Second Epistle of Paul The Apostle to the Corinthians, and the Epistles to Timothy, Titus and Philemon* [Edinburgh: Oliver and Boyd, 1964], p. 396). Philemon is already reaping the spiritual reward of a loving and faithful heart! Paul again uses the same word for *love—agape—*to describe how he feels for Philemon, as he has used to describe Philemon's attitude towards his own brothers and sisters in Christ. He knows that he is writing to a man who is motivated by love. The word *appeal* in the Greek is transliterated *parakaleo*, meaning "to call near, invite, invoke (by imploration, exhortation, or consolation) (*Strong's Exhaustive Concordance of the Bible* [Peabody: Hendrickson Publishers, 1890], Word #3870). Paul was about to extend an invitation— an opportunity for Philemon to act in kindness.

Notice that Paul also makes a couple of statements about himself: that he is aged, and that he is in prison. This could have softened Philemon's heart even more. Although Paul wasn't that old (about 60 at the time), the years had taken their toll. He had endured persecutions, floggings, and hardships in all his travels. He had a "thorn in the flesh" that God would not remove (2 Cor. 12:7). So the years that Paul lived packed a punch, and Paul was appealing to him by reminding him of the difficulties he had endured in the faith.

ᴄᴡ An Invitation to Forgive

And yet Paul respects Philemon's free will. In doing so, we see a very practical application in how to graciously encourage someone to forgive.

He reminds Philemon that he is to forgive not only because it is God's command, but seeks to inspire him to forgive from the heart. We could say that what was delivered to Philemon was an invitation to compassion.

Paul then comes out and states his appeal to Philemon:

> *10) I appeal to you for my son Onesimus, whom I have begotten while in my chains."*

❤ What do you think you would do if you were in Philemon's sandals? You are holding a letter from Paul with a gentle challenge to you, and the person you are to forgive is right in front of you?

_____

_____

_____

❤ Have you ever received a similar appeal to forgive a loved one? How did it affect you?

_____

_____

_____

❤ What do you think Paul would do if Philemon does not accept his invitation to forgive?

_____

_____

_____

In this chapter, we've discussed Paul's appeal to Philemon and how the bond of love between the two of them could influence Philemon to act mercifully towards Onesimus. For someone with Philemon's character, this was bound to make an impact. However, there is an even greater impact on another character mentioned in this book—the change within Onesimus himself when he received <u>eternal</u> forgiveness in Christ. There is much to be said for this transformation, so we'll take a look at this in our next chapter.

4

The Transformation of The One Forgiven

"Who once was unprofitable to you, but now is profitable to you and to me. 12) I am sending him back. You therefore receive him, that is, my own heart, 13) whom I wished to keep with me, that on your behalf he might minister to me in my chains for the gospel"

Onesimus wasn't Paul's physical son, but a spiritual son because he was brought to faith and repentance through his encounter with Paul. So here we have a spiritually free man in physical chains who brought a physically free man out of spiritual chains. How wonderful is that? Paul uses this fatherly, loving term in reference to those younger men who were closest to him—Timothy, Titus, and others. He states that Onesimus was "once unprofitable to you, but now is profitable to you and me." The NIV states *"was useless to you... become useful...."* Why would he say that? He is telling Philemon that Onesimus is not the same person. He was now a brother in Christ, and a transformation had taken place in Onesimus that would radically have an effect on his service and relationship to Philemon. How would becoming a believer in Christ affect Onesimus's usefulness to Philemon? Let's look at just some of the things that come to mind:

ONESIMUS NOW HAD A NEW NATURE

When we accept Christ as our Lord and Savior, the Bible says that we are given a new nature.

> *You, however, did not come to know Christ that way. Surely you heard of him and were taught in him in accordance with the truth that is in Jesus. You were taught, with regard to your former way of life, to put off your old self, which is being*

The Transformation of The One Forgiven

corrupted by its deceitful desires; to be made new in the attitude of your minds; and to put on the new self, created to be like God in true righteousness and holiness (Eph. 4:20–24 NIV).

Let's look at how that is actually evidenced in the believer's life by reading the following Scriptures and completing the chart below:

What do these say about the Old Nature?	Contrast with the New Nature.
Romans 8:8:	Col. 1:10:
Romans 6:6:	Romans 6:7:
Romans 8:5–6:	Romans 8:5–6:

Onesimus may have been a slave by trade, but now he was free in the best possible way. He was free to choose righteousness. Sin no longer was his true master (Rom. 6:22).

How do you think Onesimus's new nature would affect his life and relationship to Philemon?

_____

_____

_____

An Invitation to Forgive

ONESIMUS COULD NOW HAVE A NEW PERSPECTIVE IN HIS WORK

Read Col. 3:22–25:

> *Bondservants, obey in all things your masters according to the flesh, not with eyeservice, as men-pleasers, but in sincerity of heart, fearing God. And whatever you do, do it heartily, as to the Lord and not to men, knowing that from the Lord you will receive the reward of the inheritance; for you serve the Lord Christ. But he who does wrong will be repaid for what he has done, and there is no partiality.*

It is no wonder this phrase was included in the book of Colossians, for it was also read to the Church at Colosse along with the letter of Philemon. I wouldn't doubt that Paul had Onesimus in mind when he wrote it. This was Onesimus's new mandate and new perspective as a slave. Now, every time he was serving Philemon, he was serving the Lord. He wasn't just going to work when Philemon was looking, as eyeservice. Instead, he would work out of his love for the Lord, and he knew that he was gaining his reward from the Lord. This is in contrast to the unregenerate man (the unbeliever) in Ecc. 2:22–23—*"For what has man for all his labor, and for the striving of his heart with which he has toiled under the sun? For all his days are sorrowful, and his work burdensome; even in the night his heart takes no rest. This also is vanity."* Solomon, the author of Ecclesiastes, is saying, "What's the point?" On our own resource and strength, there is no joy in work, no purpose. Sure, it may have value in a mortal sense, but if it isn't done as unto the Lord, it has no eternal meaning.

The Transformation of The One Forgiven

Read Col. 3:23 and paraphrase in your own words:

_____
_____
_____
_____

Wow! Did you know that we will receive a just, eternal compensation for our earthly efforts, regardless of how we are compensated here on earth? What a perspective! How do you think that must have affected Onesimus's service to Philemon?

_____
_____
_____
_____

What about you and me? Granted, we are not "bondslaves," but the terminology can be applied to our submission to superiors in the workplace, and even in the home as we consider ourselves to be submissive one to another (Eph. 5:21).

♥ When we perform in our occupations, do we consider that when we work for our superiors, we are really working for the Lord as Paul described in this passage? Can you give an example from your own life?

_____
_____
_____
_____

ᴖ An Invitation to Forgive

Onesimus was useful for ministry

Read ahead a little to verses 12–13:

> *"I am sending him back. You therefore receive him, that is, my own heart, whom I wished to keep with me, that on your behalf he might minister to me in my chains for the gospel."*

As a brother in Christ, Onesimus ministered to Paul. He was an asset to the Apostle to the degree that Paul wanted to keep him around, even though it was ripping Paul's heart out to send him back. He implies that to have Onesimus back would be a welcome gift. Onesimus was loved and valuable enough that Paul could mention him as one who could act on Philemon's behalf. Now that's a compliment! (Not to mention another wonderful persuasion to Philemon!) He had been transformed by Christ to be useful to Paul, not necessarily in terms of the typical assistance of a slave, but in the greater terms of furthering the kingdom of God.

♥ Can you think of a time when a fellow believer or group of believers ministered to you when you most needed it? They were being useful to the kingdom of God!

_____

_____

The Transformation of The One Forgiven

♥ In what ways can you think of that you can minister to other fellow believers? What ways are you useful to the body of Christ? If you are not actively serving a body of believers, can you think of ways that God can use your gifts and talents to minister to others in your present world?

_____

_____

Having examined the character of the one who forgives, and the transformation of the one forgiven, we move now to consider the dynamics of forgiveness.

5
The Dynamics of Forgiveness

"But without your consent I wanted to do nothing, that your good deed might not be by compulsion, as it were, but voluntary."

Paul doesn't want to keep Onesimus against Philemon's will nor does he want to demand that Philemon forgive Onesimus. What does this tell us about the dynamics of forgiveness? Well, several things:

Dynamic #1 - The Selflessness Of The Mediator

Paul was respectful of the resource Philemon already had in Onesimus. He had the presence of mind to see more at play in God's plan than to presume that God had provided Onesimus to be at his own (Paul's) service. As mediators of forgiveness, we must check our hearts to see that our own desires and preferences do not oppose God's purposes. Even when we are called just to give advice between two people, we must be careful not to rely on our own leanings and bias.

What a principle! Here Paul is in chains and probably in need of some type of helpmate while in prison. Onesimus comes along and has proven himself useful; even a blessing to Paul. What a joy he must have been to Paul! It would be so easy for Paul to assume that God had provided Onesimus for himself. On the surface, the assumption would have been a noble one. He would have been furthering the kingdom of God! Yet, in a most selfless manner, Paul sees the bigger purpose and plan of God and would not stand in the way of its fulfillment. We can see that Paul cared more about the reconciling work of God between Philemon and Onesimus than his own needs.

The Dynamics of Forgiveness

💗 Have you ever been in a circumstance that may have appeared to you to be God's will, but may not have been the course He would have wanted for you? Give an example.

_____

_____

_____

_____

How do you think Paul's actions reflect his trust in God?

_____

_____

_____

_____

Let's allow this to speak to us personally. I don't know about you, but sometimes we can get so caught up in our own little world that we forget what is more at stake; that is, the family, friends, and acquaintances whose needs we can meet and in whom God has already started to work His purpose. As much as you or I may want it to be, our lives aren't about what we may want for ourselves. It isn't about what can be gained from a situation or how God can bless exclusively. It's about the greater purposes of God within the situations that we encounter.

Perhaps a little perspective is in order. How can we consider the needs of others in a particular circumstance? Pause now to ask the Lord to give you a broader perspective on your relationships according to His purpose. What might He presently desire for your children or spouse? What is the greater need that would be met through a selfless act on your part? What decision do you need to make that would best fall in line with Biblical principles?

💜   Take the time necessary to ask the Lord to bring it to mind, and feel free to write your thoughts and prayers as He leads.

_____

_____

_____

_____

Dynamic #2 – The Active Participation Of The One Who Forgives

Paul wanted Philemon's forgiveness to be genuine. Had Paul kept Onesimus with him, Philemon never would have been face to face with Onesimus. It would have been easy for Philemon to be off the hook. Certainly, Philemon could have said he had forgiven Onesimus from a distance, but now that Onesimus would be in Philemon's presence, Onesimus was in Philemon's hands. He had the chance to punish him if he wanted to. What would he do with him now that he had him back? Needless to day, Philemon's heart was truly being tested.

The story of the prodigal son is such a wonderful example of active forgiveness (Luke 15:11–32). It is a story of a son that decides to foolishly squander an early inheritance and ends up in poverty. He realizes that even the servants in his father's house lived better than he was living at that point and decides to humbly return to his father for forgiveness. His father could have been reluctant to forgive him, but instead he welcomes him with joy. We are told in Scripture that as his son was approaching the father and while he was "still a great way off," the father came running to meet him. He didn't wait for the son to even come close. He ran to him with open arms. That's the picture of a forgiving heart!

I believe that God desires that we obey and live out our faith moved and motivated by our love for Him and not out of compulsion, as in the law. We are now not obligated by the law, but free to fulfill the law because his precepts are within us, a part of our hearts. *"For this is the covenant that I will make with the house of Israel after those days, says the Lord, I will put My laws in their mind and write them on their hearts; and I will be their God, and they will be My people"* (Heb. 8:10). What a difference it makes to comply with godly principles when it is written in your heart as a believer, unlike the days of the law, which only brought the knowledge of sin (Rom. 3:20).

Would you agree with the following statement, "Under constraint there is no opportunity to show free willingness to do what is required"? Why or why not?

_____

_____

_____

_____

Do you believe that forgiveness requires action? Yes ____ No ____.

DYNAMIC #3 – THE ACTIVE REPENTANCE OF THE ONE WHO NEEDS FORGIVENESS

Paul wanted Philemon to see that Onesimus was repentant. How do we know that he was? Well, he proved it by being of service to Paul, but more importantly, because he went back to Philemon!

ॐ An Invitation to Forgive

Colossians 4:7–9 records Paul's comments to the Colossians that he is sending *"Tychicus...with Onesimus, a faithful and beloved brother, who is one of you..."* back to Philemon and his household. Onesimus took a risk in facing Philemon. We know that he must have been extremely humble to be willing to do that.

In Matthew 3:7–8 (NIV), John the Baptist rebukes the Pharisees for their legalism and outward religious appearance without substance. He admonished them to "produce fruit in keeping with repentance." What do you think John the Baptist was talking about? Do you see the "fruit of repentance" demonstrated in Onesimus?

_____

_____

_____

_____

Take a moment to read Matt. 5:24, for it addresses this point well. Even if you are at the altar, the Scripture says, *"Remember that your brother has something against you, leave your offering there before the alter and go; first be reconciled to your brother, and then come and present your offering"* (Matt. 5:23–24 NASB).

❤ Have you ever felt conviction to pursue reconciliation in a relationship to the point that you dropped everything to reach out to the other person? If so, please describe.

_____

_____

_____

_____

Notice that the Scripture (Matt. 5:23) addresses the one that has created the offense, not the offended. Don't just assume that he has forgiven you or that everything is okay. Go to him. That's what Onesimus decided to do. He expressed his desire to reconcile by returning. That's what the prodigal son did, too. His repentance required a deliberate decision demonstrated by action.

Do you believe that repentance requires action? Yes ____ No ____.

Forgiveness and repentance aren't easy in themselves. Everyone involved had a difficulty to overcome. Thankfully, the testimony of their lives proved faithful as an example of the power of the Holy Spirit working so perfectly within them.

As we've taken a close look at these men's hearts, we've seen God's work in them as individuals. We will now discover the big picture that goes beyond the individual to see how God orchestrated His purposes among them.

6
THE PURPOSES OF GOD

"For perhaps he departed for a while for this purpose, that you might receive him forever, 16) no longer as a slave but more than a slave—a beloved brother, especially to me but how much more to you, both in the flesh and in the Lord."

Paul makes some profound statements here concerning Onesimus. When we consider what the Holy Spirit has inspired him to mention, we can realize that they resonate to any "Onesimus" we may know today. Consider just a few items that are implied in this verse:

The Providence Of God

> *"For perhaps he departed for a while for this purpose, that you might receive him forever."*

In verses 12–13, Paul tells Philemon that it is more important that he is sending Onesimus back for the purpose of reconciling him to Philemon. Now he is making a statement about why he believes Onesimus departed at all—that he (by the providence of God) would come to saving faith in Christ. Paul is saying, "Philemon, maybe this is what it took for him to come to Christ. Maybe he wouldn't have come to know salvation if he had not stolen and ran away at all. What he did wasn't right, but now this temporary hardship has resulted in eternal purpose."

The Purposes of God

As believers, we know that God is always working in our lives (Romans 8:28). He doesn't just put things in motion and stand at a distance to see what happens. This is the deep contentment and mystery to His secret providence of our lives. Consider this great truth: God is our heavenly Father. He does and will work in everything, even our mistakes. Glory to God for this! To His great praise, He allows us to fall so that we can learn from our mistakes. He uses the temporary rebellion of His children or children-to-be for our good and for His glory.

The Bible is full of great examples. Consider Jonah, who did everything he could to run from God. He got on a boat headed the opposite way from where God told him to go. God humbled him and used him to lead the city of Nineveh to Himself (see the book of Jonah).

How about the Apostle Peter? He had some rough edges—Christ allowed him to be greatly tested (Luke 22:31). The result? He became one of the greatest Apostles and leaders of the New Testament Church.

How about the story of Joseph and his brothers? They despised Joseph as a boy, and maliciously threw him into a pit to die. Instead, he was picked up by an Egyptian caravan. He eventually found himself in a position to use his gifts and abilities to warn the Egyptians of a famine in the land. God used his brothers' rebellion and hatred for the good of many, and brought them all to an overwhelming transformation of heart and joyous reunion with Joseph. Joseph forgave them, saying, *"But as for you, you meant evil against me; but God meant it for good, in order to bring it about as it is this day, to save many people alive"* (Gen. 50:20).

Paul himself was speaking out of experience. Paul was the self-confessed "worst of sinners," (1 Timothy 1:15–16), a righteous Pharisee who made it his life's mission to persecute and kill Christians before he was dramatically confronted by Christ Himself (Acts 9). God used the years of rebellion and evil to help fuel his humility and zeal for God, and Paul became one of the greatest Apostles ever known. So God used Onesimus's rebellion to give Philemon the opportunity and joy of forgiveness, not to mention a new brother in Christ. For Onesimus, the plan he contrived for evil was used as the event that led to his conversion.

As Paul considers God's purpose above his own desires when he let Onesimus go back to Philemon, he encourages Philemon to consider God's purpose above his own anger to Onesimus as he receives him back. Why would Philemon hinder God's will, which was already set in motion?

Friend, do you know an Onesimus? Is he your child, husband or wife? Is your "Onesimus" a dear friend who is turning his back on God? Please know that the same God that brought the saints back to Himself, who never left them and died on the cross for them is the same One that you know. That is reassuring to me; I hope that it is as reassuring to you as well. Pray for that loved one and know that our God is a God of second chances. Maybe you have not seen the good from the evil in your loved one yet, but by the providence of God, we have the hope of His restoration. As one of my Sunday school teachers once said, "He is a God of 'do-overs.'"

Do you need a do-over? By virtue of your repentance, you have already begun to reap the restoration. Chances are, if you have turned back to the Lord after a period of rebellion, God has already done a great work in your life. Chances are that he has providentially put people in your life to steer you back to him. You may have asked yourself the same question that Paul asked the Romans, *"What fruit did you have then in the things of which you are now ashamed? For the end of those things is death"* (Romans 6:21). What does it profit to sin? Your testimony can and will be used to benefit others if you are open and available to share it.

❤ Can you recall a circumstance that was meant for evil in your life that God turned out for the good?

_____

_____

_____

Take comfort from God's faithfulness despite man's rebellion. He is faithful to forgive and use our mistakes for good. This never means that we can take His kindness for granted and use it as an excuse to sin again. Instead, let us be grateful for His forgiveness and decide to obey the next time around!

THE CHRISTIAN LIFE CAN BE LIVED IN ANY CIRCUMSTANCE

> *"... no longer as a slave but more than a slave—a beloved brother, especially to me but how much more to you, both in the flesh and in the Lord."*

Note the next several words. Paul never sought Onesimus's freedom as a slave. The New Living Translation (NLT) states, ***"He is no longer just a slave; he is a beloved brother...."*** Paul's point is not to approve of slavery, but that Onesimus had the ability to live a Christian life no matter what circumstance he was in. Of course, if given the opportunity to be free, he should be free, but the point was that he was to grow where he was planted.

In 1 Cor. 7:20–24 (NASB 1995), Paul says,

> *Each man must remain in that condition in which he was called. Were you called while a slave? Do not worry about it; but if you are able also to become free, rather do that. For he who was called in the Lord while a slave, is the Lord's freedman; likewise he who was called while free, is Christ's slave. You were bought with a price; do not become slaves of men. Brethren, each one is to remain with God in that condition in which he was called.*

John MacArthur comments,

> Paul made no distinction. Any slave, in any circumstance, was to be willing to remain as he was. Only sin can keep us from obeying and serving the Lord, circumstance cannot. Therefore if we are in a difficult, uncomfortable, and restricting situation, we should not worry about it, but should determine to be faithful as long as the Lord leaves us there (*The MacArthur New Testament Commentary, 1 Corinthians* [Chicago: The Moody Bible Institute, 1984] p. 174).

He goes on to mention,

> However it is that we have been saved (called), and in whatever condition we now are in, we should be willing to remain. God allows us to be where we are and to stay where we are for a purpose. Conversion is not the signal for a person to leave his social condition, his marriage or his singleness, his human master, or his other circumstances. We are to leave

sin and anything that encourages sin; but otherwise we are to stay where we are until God moves us (*The MacArthur New Testament Commentary, 1 Corinthians* [Chicago: The Moody Bible Institute, 1984], p. 175).

Let us also remember that Paul himself was in jail, and even so was a minister to everyone around him.

♥ Beloved, does this principle speak to you? Do you find your occupation or place in life unfulfilling? Do you sometimes wish you were somewhere else or doing something else? Please know that you can be effective for the Lord right where you are. Remember, Onesimus was immediately useful to Paul, even as a new believer. How many people do you know that are dying apart from the Lord, that may work right next to you? How about the customers that come to your business, or the homemaker across the street? Give examples below.

_____

_____

_____

_____

You may be able to reach those folks that perhaps your Sunday school teacher or pastor never could, whether you are new to the faith or not! God is faithful to equip us to thrive where He has placed us, and you can be assured that He has given you all that you need for life and godliness (2 Peter 1:3).

Sometimes we lose heart at the ungodliness around us. We wish we were in an environment that was more honoring to the Lord and find ourselves complaining and belly-aching about it. We want to work with other like-minded believers at church, or some ministry, but is it rational to think that we should be moved from our present circumstance? We can't all be pastors or missionaries!

❤ Write your own prayer to the Lord about where He has taken you thus far. Thank Him for His providence and the unique privilege He has given you to thrive and to minister to those He has put in your present life and circumstances. Ask Him to heighten your awareness of any opportunity to share His love and truth. He is every bit as providential in your life as He was in Onesimus's!

_____

_____

_____

_____

THE FELLOWSHIP OF THE FAITH

"…No longer as a slave but more than a slave – a beloved brother, especially to me but how much more to you, both in the flesh and in the Lord." (v. 16). Onesimus could now share in this "fellowship of faith" that Paul mentioned earlier. There was now a like-mindedness between Philemon and Onesimus, and with the church at Colosse. As Onesimus moved about Philemon's household, he must have come into contact with the church at Philemon's home. He wouldn't have understood the knowledge of God or the faith of those that met there, but he must have sensed the joy among them (v. 7). Did he feel like an outsider? Now that he was a believer, he was more of an insider. He could serve Philemon not only in an earthly capacity but also as one in regards to eternal purpose. He was one of the family of faith.

The Purposes of God

Read Colossians 4:7–9.

This is the final greeting Paul writes to the Colossians. Remember, this book was also sent back with Tychicus and Onesimus, and was probably read at the same time as the book of Philemon.

What does Paul call Onesimus (v. 9)? Faithful and beloved _____, who is _____ of you. They (Onesimus and Tychicus) will _____.

So, we see in Philemon 15 a picture of God's providence. We see His purpose for and within Onesimus specifically. He used his rebellion as the crossroads of his life, to bring him to faith. He made his transformation useful within the circumstances he was already in, and He provided Onesimus with a family of faith with which to belong and serve.

Paul now begins to write even more compelling text that I am sure moved Philemon's heart. They are rich and full of insight into the heart of Paul, which we'll discuss in our next lesson.

7

The Motives of One Who Forgives

"If then you count me as a partner, receive him as you would me. 18) But if he has wronged you or owes anything, put that on my account. 19) I, Paul, am writing with my own hand. I will repay—not to mention to you that you owe me even your own self besides. 20) Yes, brother, let me have joy from you in the Lord; refresh my heart in the Lord. 21) Having confidence in your obedience, I write to you, knowing that you will do even more than I say. 22) But meanwhile, also prepare a guest room for me, for I trust that through your prayers I shall be granted to you."

As we near the end of this rich letter, we come upon several passages that strongly indicate the motives of one who forgives. They are expressed in Paul's appeals to Philemon:

Motivation #1 – We Are All One In Christ

> *"If then you count me as a partner, receive him as you would me" (v. 17).*

Paul steps into Onesimus's place. He tells Philemon that if he considers him (Paul) a partner, then receive Onesimus as well. He's saying, "If you receive me, then receive him, too. Treat him as you would me." Paul was Onesimus's spiritual mentor, encouraging and refreshing him. He is saying, "Refresh him, too." It's important to encourage the ones older in the faith, but how much more those who are new to the faith? He is an example to Philemon on how to treat Onesimus. They were one in Christ now. Knowing how much Paul meant to Philemon, this directive would certainly have been hard to resist.

THE MOTIVES OF ONE WHO FORGIVES

Do you see others as equal in the body of Christ, regardless of race, appearance, status, or maturity in the faith? What about those who have had a colorful past? How do we honestly treat them? The way we treat them reflects our commitment to the welfare of the church.

Read James 2:1–9. In your own words, what is this passage saying? Consider the church you attend. Do you see any partiality in your group? Do you see any subtle (or not so subtle) cliques? What do you think can be done to come to terms with this?

_____

_____

_____

_____

MOTIVATION #2 – THE OFFERING OF RESTITUTION

> *"But if he has wronged you or owes anything, put that on my account" (v. 18).*

Although he pleaded Onesimus's case, Paul did not sweep the offense under the rug. He didn't pretend as though it never happened. That does not teach the sinner nor does it acknowledge the one offended. As long as we are in this fallen world, sin will always be a reality. Let no man deceive you. Sin is real, and it has a price. There is always a spiritual separation from God (Romans 6:23), if not logical consequences. Further, it is always a biblical theme that there must be restitution for sin. Always. Throughout the Old Testament, animals had to die as sacrifices for daily atonement for sin until Christ, the ultimate sacrifice, came and died once and for all (Heb. 10:10). Paul is acting upon this principle—not that Onesimus wasn't already forgiven by God through his position in Christ, but that sin had consequences for which Paul was ready to step in and rectify.

Some churches today won't even acknowledge sin because they are afraid it will offend someone. Nonsense! Sin is real. We cannot know the good news of the gospel until we understand the bad news that we are sinners, in need of a Savior. First John says, *"If we say that we have no sin, we deceive ourselves, and the truth is not in us. If we confess our sins, He is faithful and just to forgive us our sins, and to cleanse us from all unrighteousness"* (1:8–9, KJV). The most loving thing we can do for a brother in Christ is to acknowledge the reality of sin. We are to hate the sin, but love the sinner. Paul was acting Christlike in his willingness to step in and pay the price Onesimus stole.

MOTIVATION #3 – THE FORGIVENESS WE HAVE ALREADY BEEN GIVEN

> *"I, Paul, am writing with my own hand. I will repay—not to mention to you that you owe me even your own self besides"* (v. 19).

Sometimes throughout Scripture as we read of Paul's travels and ministry, we also get a glimpse of his sharp and witty personality intermingled with the truth of what is being said. This is such a classic example. As if all that Paul has already said to persuade Philemon to take Onesimus back (the compliment, the benefits of forgiveness,

The Motives of One Who Forgives

the relationship he had to Paul, the respect he gives Philemon, the reminder of God's providence, and the offer of restitution) weren't enough, it is as if Paul is saying, "Here are all these reasons to take Onesimus back, but in case you've forgotten, you owe me your own life besides."

Wow! Sometimes so much can be said with so few words! Paul brought Philemon to the Lord at Ephesus—that was the most priceless gift anyone could offer. He was indebted to Paul—what Onesimus owed him was nothing in comparison, and whatever that was, Paul was proving his authenticity by signing for it himself with his own hand.

Look up the following Scriptures and answer the questions below:

Ephesians 4:32—If God forgives us, how is it that we can't forgive a relatively small debt others owe us?

_____

_____

_____

_____

Matthew 6:12—Remembering what we owe Christ, what is our attitude?

_____

_____

_____

_____

ᛜ An Invitation to Forgive

Considering how much and how often we have been forgiven, what would you say ought to be our response to those who have done something against us?

_____

_____

_____

_____

A great illustration of this precept is described in a most memorable parable concerning forgiveness. Please read Matthew 18:23–35.

Who do the following represent in this parable? The master represents _____, the evil servant represents _____, and the fellow servant represents _____.

It's so easy to get in a huff about the evil servant and wonder why he couldn't forgive a small debt, when he was forgiven so much, but that's exactly what we all do when we don't forgive our fellow man. Seeing the discrepancy between what Onesimus owed Philemon, and what Philemon owed Paul, it could be said that what Paul is really saying to Philemon is to charge it to his account, and then cancel it. I love Paul's example here because it can have such a practical application in our prayers. Couldn't we also approach God and ask that any offense be charged to Christ's account? We acknowledge that He died for the individual that hurt us, knowing that He is capable of righting the wrong done to us. I believe it is every bit in God's character to remind us of all we owe Him and move us to cancel any vindictive motive. While an offender may be moved towards restitution and may want to repay, we can accept it, but we have the freedom in Christ to cancel the emotional or literal debt, if there is one.

Motivation #4 – The Joy It Will Give Others

> *"Yes, brother, let me have joy from you in the Lord; refresh my heart in the Lord"* (v. 20).

When we forgive, it stands as a testimony to others. Paul has already told Philemon (vv. 4–7) what a blessing he is to others, and now he is asking for that same joy for himself when and if he hears of Philemon's right actions. This implies that if he didn't forgive Onesimus, it would sadden and grieve Paul. Again, Paul is encouraging Philemon to give back a portion of the joy he has experienced as a result of his salvation, that is, to show Paul that not a bit of what he has invested in Philemon was in vain.

Motivation #5 – Obedience

> *"…having confidence in your obedience, I write to you, knowing that you will do even more than I say"* (v. 21).

Sometimes it comes down to pure obedience, doesn't it? As we discussed earlier, a heart of forgiveness often starts with obedience. Philemon was familiar with God's principles of forgiveness; he was already a believer. If we have been believers for long, we know enough about God's Word to follow through with it by application and not just by hearing it.

An Invitation to Forgive

Read James 1:22–25. What does this passage say about one who is a doer of the Word?

_____

_____

_____

_____

We can only speculate on what Paul was implying when he writes *"knowing that you will do even more than what I say"* (v. 21). Considering verse 15, we know it couldn't be Onesimus's emancipation. Perhaps it was giving Onesimus greater duties and service as now he was a brother in Christ. Perhaps it was in reference to canceling the debt he owed. The idea here is that Paul expected Philemon to welcome Onesimus in love and acceptance, to not just forgive, but to treat him with kindness.

Motivation #6 – Accountability

> *"But meanwhile, also prepare a guest room for me, for I trust that through your prayers I shall be granted to you"* (v. 22).

Earlier Paul created accountability by mention of the church; this time it is through an anticipated action. He asks Philemon to prepare a room for him, and states that he is trusting that God will answer Philemon's prayers for his (Paul's) release. He is essentially telling Philemon that he is planning on coming to see him, Lord willing, and he's going to find out what has happened.

How does Paul expect that Onesimus should be set free? Through Philemon's prayers. This puts Philemon in a bit of a bind. Again, John MacArthur has some wonderful insight, especially on this passage. He observes,

> Paul literally paints him into a corner. [Paul says] 'I'm coming and I'm expecting that what will free me is your prayers.' That's a heavy burden. Now Philemon is saying to himself, '…If I don't pray, he doesn't get out of prison…I don't want to be responsible for him being in prison, I've got to pray for his release, I'm praying for his release, I know where his first stop is…here, I've got to forgive him [Onesimus].' That's spiritual accountability' ("The Motives of one who Forgives" [Transcript of Tape GC 57-4, 1997], p. 7).

Write down James 5:16. How do you see this Scripture as it pertains to accountability?

_____
_____
_____
_____

◈ An Invitation to Forgive

Can you recall a time when God moved and worked His purposes through your answered prayer?

_____

_____

_____

_____

8
As Examples

"Epaphras, my fellow prisoner in Christ Jesus, greets you, 24) as do Mark, Aristarchus, Demas, Luke, my fellow laborers. 25) The grace of our Lord Jesus Christ be with your spirit. Amen."

In closing, Paul mentions the greetings of five men who are beloved of him and of Philemon himself.

Epaphras, described as a "fellow prisoner in Christ Jesus" was probably the founder of the Church at Colosse. He came to Rome because he was concerned about heresy in the church and stayed behind with Paul at the time of the writing of Philemon. Of course, hosting the church at Colosse, Philemon knew Epaphras as a leader, not only because he sought the purity of the church by consulting Paul, but because he was *"a bondservant of Christ...always laboring fervently for [the church] in prayers, that [they] may stand perfect and complete in all the will of God"* (Col. 4:12).

Mark is the second one mentioned, and I think the most compelling, given the fact that Paul himself was once at odds with him, and more specifically with Barnabas, his cousin.

Please read the story found in Acts 15:36–41.

Mark was supposed to join Barnabas and Paul on a journey to Pamphylia but could not deal with the difficulties involved and deserted them on the way. Later, as Paul and Barnabas were planning a second missionary journey to retrace the first, Paul and Barnabas got into a heated argument about whether to include Mark. Paul insisted that Mark had his chances and he would not receive him back. Barnabas wanted Mark to come along. The Scripture says that the contention became so sharp that they parted ways. Whatever became of Paul's relationship to Mark?

Read on to 2 Tim. 4:11 in the NASB (1995)—What does Paul say about Mark? "...Pick up Mark and bring him with you, for he is _____ to me for service."

Paul was writing to Timothy from his 2nd imprisonment in Rome. By this time (and really by the time of his present imprisonment), two things had happened. One, Mark had improved so greatly that he was considered faithful and useful to the ministry. He was no longer the guy that ran at the first difficulty. He was a godly and useful servant. In fact, he wrote the Gospel of Mark. How do you think this influenced Philemon? Does this sound very similar to Philemon's dilemma? If Mark knew any of Philemon's story, he could encourage Philemon himself. "Philemon, I was like Onesimus; I've been there. Give the guy a second chance." Secondly, Paul had forgiven Mark. Seems the Apostle himself had his own dealings with forgiveness and reconciliation and could write not only from the leading of the Holy Spirit but also from an understanding of what it meant to forgive.

Aristarchus is mentioned as Paul's fellow prisoner in Col. 4:10, but as a fellow laborer in the book of Philemon. Remembering that these two books were sent back to Colosse at the same time, we could conclude that Aristarchus was a fellow prisoner by choice, simply willingly attached to the imprisonment of Paul to assist him. He was a Macedonian from Thessalonica (Acts 27:2) and a traveling companion to Paul (Acts 20:4). He was also willing to suffer for Christ because it is noted that he was seized at the riot of Ephesus (Acts 19:29).

Demas was also with Paul while he was in this present imprisonment. He appeared to be an associate of Paul's, but in his later writing to Timothy, we see that he ended up forsaking Paul entirely, "having loved this present world..." (2 Tim. 4:10). Yet Paul was willing to forgive him (and others) who did him harm, saying, "...may it not be charged against them" (2 Tim. 4:16). Remarkable! Paul was in the business of forgiving. He reconciled with Mark, counting him worthy of service, and would also ask for God's grace over Demas.

Lastly, Luke is mentioned. Besides being the author of the Gospel of Luke and Acts, one of his most prominent characteristics was his faithfulness to Paul. He stuck by him in his travels and both Roman imprisonments, up until the time of Paul's execution. In the same passage of Second Timothy, Paul tells Timothy that after everyone else departed from him for one reason or another, only Luke remained (2 Tim. 4:11).

With the exception of Demas (who was not even found out to be a quitter at the time), we are talking about some incredible men of God who were in fellowship with Philemon. They were saints who were great fellow-laborers, each with their own hardships and persecutions. Philemon is reminded of his own "great cloud of witnesses," so to speak (Heb. 12:1). Their lives attested to the fact that the Christian life was not easy, and that each of us has a role in encouraging and holding each other accountable in the fellowship. Mark's seasonal immaturity affected his relationship to Paul, and that affected Paul's relationship to Barnabas and their ministry together. Demas unfortunately had a negative effect on Paul's ministry, breaking their fellowship. Was Philemon going to do the same? Would he disappoint or would he refresh the brethren? Did he realize that his actions were not in isolation but would affect those around him or that knew him? Would he step up to the plate quickly and willingly, or would he somehow create another conflict in relationship?

As Examples

❤ Have you ever watched a movie that took the same characters and re-arranged their lives, showing how different they would be had they made one decision differently? No doubt, I know that God is sovereign, and His will and purpose will be accomplished no matter what. I also believe that all things work together for good to those that love the Lord and are called according to his purposes (Romans 8:28), but sometimes our flesh nature can cause us to learn the hard way, can't it? What do you think we will reap if we don't stop to consider how our actions and words can easily affect others?

_____

_____

_____

_____

❤ Read 1 Corinthians 12:26. Have you personally seen this dynamic played out in the body of Christ? Please share an example.

_____

_____

_____

_____

Just in speculation, what do you think would have resulted if Philemon chose not to forgive Onesimus?

_____

_____

_____

_____

An Invitation to Forgive

Our impulsive and prideful human nature is the reason Paul reminds Philemon of one last thing: He needs the grace of God to do this.

> *"The grace of our Lord Jesus Christ be with your spirit. Amen" (v. 25).*

Paul weighed his words with Philemon. He never hindered God's work, but recognized His providence as he set himself aside and spoke the truth in love. He didn't take the opportunity to keep Onesimus for himself nor did he lash out at Philemon. As a result, how do you think Paul affected the body of Christ?

_____

_____

_____

_____

Well, did Philemon actually forgive Onesimus? We are never told, but I believe he must have. Bible scholars will tell you that it's not likely that this book would have made it to the New Testament Canon if he didn't, because it would have given human history a false impression of Philemon. If Philemon hadn't forgiven Onesimus, and the early churches knew it, what type of testimony would it have given them? What's more, it is recorded in church history through a letter from the Christian leader Ignatius, that some time after this, a man became the pastor of the church at Ephesus and his name was Onesimus (John MacArthur, *Twelve Unlikely Heroes* [Nashville, Tennessee: Thomas Nelson, 2012], p. 208). Could it have been the same man? If it was, you can imagine the impact that one decision must have made!

What a lot we have covered! The applications are so many because we all have to deal with the issue of forgiveness. I don't know if Paul knew that his personal letter would have such a huge effect, but among so much more, we learn such truths: You can't run away from your problems; only freely offered sacrifices are pleasing to God; a soft answer takes away strife. Most of all, we gain much needed insight on the beauty of forgiveness since there isn't one of us who has not needed to forgive, be forgiven, or mediate reconciliation. May the grace of God be with you.

Discussion Questions—Character Studies

Philemon:

Are you challenged to be more like Philemon? It isn't easy to forgive, but from his life, we can understand what a forgiving person looks like. What about his character do you most admire? Was it his love for Christ and the saints? His dedication to the church? His refreshing countenance? Or his compassion for Paul and Onesimus?

_____

_____

_____

_____

❧ An Invitation to Forgive

What great rewards and benefits come with being a forgiving person?

_____
_____
_____
_____

Paul:

What most inspired you about how Paul communicated to Philemon? Is there anything about his wisdom that is particularly applicable to your life right now?

_____
_____
_____
_____

What points/comments did Paul make to encourage and appeal to Philemon towards forgiving Onesimus? How can we use them in our dealings with others, when appropriate?

_____
_____
_____

Discussion Questions—Character Studies

Onesimus:

How did his transformation make him a new man? What was evident in his life to show his new life and value?

_____

_____

_____

_____

Describe why or how you believe he became so beloved to Paul. What words would you use to describe Onesimus? Does he remind you of a new believer you know?

_____

_____

_____

_____

Made in the USA
Columbia, SC
22 September 2022